10 Effective Ways to Start Your Business With 0 Dollars

Learn the Essential Practices & Habits I Used to Start My Business While Working a Full-Time Job

Natasha 'Tottie' Weston

Cover & Book Photo Credit: Jake Simpson

ISBN-13 978-0983218746

GRACE US
LIVING
PUBLICATIONS

This book is dedicated to YOU!

Continue to chase after your dreams

at any cost...

I support YOU!

Table of Contents

Introduction

Most people believe that in order to build a successful business you must have money starting out. That is not completely true. All you need is vision, passion to drive your vision and focus to stay on track. These were the basic essentials I used when I decided to pursue a career in the fashion industry. As a college dropout, living in the most "non-fashionable" state in the country, I was very limited to what was available in this field. At the time, the only things I had were my laptop, pen & paper! I didn't know anyone and to be quite honest, I had no clue where to start. After deciding that this was the career field I was determined to explore, I began to strategize and use the basic resources I had. Four years later, I can honestly write from my experiences and hope to encourage and motivate you to know that you can start your dream business with zero dollars.

In this book I will share some of my most effective practices and habits that I developed as a struggling young entrepreneur trying to start a business. Might I add, I did it all right from my mom's couch! Although the methods that I'm referring to in this book are not top government secret, they are ones that I used when I had no knowledge or strategy about business nor the industry that I was pursuing. Though I had quite a few years of college under my belt, there were just some things that not even a college textbook could teach me. What I learned was that there are many other components in starting a business, even before preparing a business plan.

Actually, I always dreamed of owning a business. Like many of you, the one thing that held me back was the lack of money and resources that I didn't have access to. This day and age, lack of money is no longer a valid excuse. With the abundance of resources available today, anyone can start building a business or brand from anywhere in the world. Unfortunately, I didn't realize this until my back was up against the wall and I was forced to research and find ways to bring my vision to life. Here I was, a young college dropout living at home with my mother. I had no job and for the first time I could remember, I never had such a hard time finding one. Though I had a lot of experience, no one was calling me. As I reflect, I am thankful that no one did at the time because I wouldn't have learned all that I did in three short years!

The bottom line is, although it helps, you don't have to have the financial means to start your own business, no matter the industry. You have to DO WHAT YOU CAN, WITH WHAT YOU HAVE, WHERE YOU ARE! My wish is that by the time you reach the last page, you will know that it is indeed possible to start building the business, brand, or career of your dreams right from your living room couch or office cubicle, and yes with 0 dollars.

Chapter One

Ask God to Show You Your Purpose

It's ironic how your God-given talent will make room for you. One day while sitting at home surfing job sites, my cousin texted me from another city asking for my help in selecting an outfit for a party. It finally dawned on me after all of the times that I've helped coordinate wardrobes for friends and family. It was at that moment, I realized that this was a passion that could potentially lead to my dream business. This life changing moment got my juices flowing and my curiosity boiling! I immediately pulled out my laptop and went to Google "fashion styling." I had no idea that this was actually a business and there were people out in the world that made lots of money doing it. Say no more, that was all I needed to know!

One of the first search results that came up was a book on how to become a fashion stylist by a well-known stylist based in Atlanta named Kim Maxwell. In her book, she takes her readers behind the scenes of a fashion stylist and shared some of the details of her journey as a fashion professional. A pivotal point that stuck out to me from her book was the importance of internships when you are trying to get into the industry. Ok, so now I was stuck with another dilemma. The reality was, I lived in South Carolina and internships in fashion weren't just flying out of the woodworks! Long story short, I had to yet again hop on the computer and do my research to find out how and where I could land an internship. Not just any internship, but one that could push me into the places I needed to be in for my vision. This was when I realized that there was a purpose to the energy that was driving me to want to search deeper into my God-given talent. I later found out that this driving energy or force was connected to me accomplishing my purpose.

We all have a purpose. It doesn't matter what your religious background, affiliation or beliefs may be. Purpose is something that we are all born with, but it's totally up to us to figure out what it is and why we have it. Without purpose, the things we do in this life have no real meaning. It seems like wasteful energy that is used in vain. Purpose is the reason why many are drawn to Oprah's generosity, President Obama's charisma, and Beyoncé's undeniable talent. Do you think these people just woke up one day and decided to be who they are? No way! They all are living out their life's purpose, and this is why the world is drawn to them. They are good at what they do because they are walking in their purpose.

Many of us never find our purpose because

we go through life just simply doing what we have been taught is the "normal" thing to do *(graduate high school and go to college to become a doctor, nurse or lawyer)*. Most of the time we chose the "safe route" because of familiarity. We are certain that jobs are guaranteed in common professions so we stay within our comfort zones, neglecting true fulfillment of purpose. When we look at past generations, very few knew what they were placed on this earth to do. Fast forward to today, this is why many are stuck in careers or doing jobs that were never apart of their life's plan.

I often look around at the people that I work with on my full-time job at the bank. Most of them are women between the ages of 30 and 65 who have been working for someone else all of their lives. Their typical day runs the same course every day and they are content. They frequently complain that they are not making enough money or that they are tired of working the same job. However, I never hear them discuss the possibility of doing something that they love and are passionate about. It's like they have no idea that they were placed on this earth for a reason and that reason may not be to work a regular 9-5 job. This has always bothered me in more ways than one. Let me be clear, most of us have to work a job to ensure that our bills get paid until we are in position to pursue our business full-time. This shouldn't be a stopping point if you want the ultimate fulfillment of working for yourself and never having to clock in and out another day of your life.

Knowing how to find your purpose is simply asking God to show you. It's like anything else in life that is not clear to you. You go straight to the source for clarity on anything you don't understand. We don't know anything until we ask the right questions. Finding out your life's purpose is no different. Although purpose is revealed to some over a length of time, asking God to show you what it is, is the very first step to building the business that will not only bring in the coins, but will also be effective. After all, your purpose is connected to a greater purpose. It should not only benefit you, because it is designed to affect those around you! The purpose of your business or vision is to make a positive difference or change in the world. If your business isn't changing your community then what good is it doing?

When I first made the decision to pursue a fashion career, I had no idea how many different aspects of the industry I would have to try and fail at. It wasn't until then that I found out where I was supposed to be and what I was supposed to be doing. As I stated earlier in this chapter, I started off wanting to be a fashion stylist. The more I engaged in the activities of the profession, I found out that fashion styling wasn't what I wanted to spend the rest of my life doing. I was supposed to only grab the knowledge and lessons learned from those particular experiences. Every discovery of what we learn is a valuable lesson. This journey sparked another discovery. It wasn't until then that I found that I had a passion for undiscovered talent in the fashion and entertainment industries. Hence the reason why I am writing this book. The thought of introducing someone's talent, business or brand to the world intrigued me. I became really effective and realized that when I took part, their brand would get a boost. My passion grew in informing and educating entrepreneurs and businesses not only on how to get in the industry but how to stay there.

This is something that I started off doing for free, and actually didn't mind doing it. This was how I began learning what my purpose was. While in pursuit to find out more, I soon found that I was able to exercise my talents through internships. An internship is when you commit your services or volunteer for a designated time period without being monetarily compensated. You learn the in's and out's while gaining knowledge of the business. Internships were a great tool in discovering what my purpose was. In fact, it was through my active involvement that ignited and pointed me in the direction to start my own company in April 2011 called Eloquence Enterprises. At that time, I had moved to New

York City for an internship with a major television network. When it didn't go as planned, I found myself doing lots of freelance work. Instead, I worked for an indie designer in New York and an established one in Los Angeles. I was also the personal assistant to an entertainment journalist. The truth was, I over extended myself and my hands were in too many cookie jars. Eventually, I figured out how to ease my hand out of some of the jars without ruining business relationships and future business connections. Keep in mind that on your journey to discovering your purpose, there will be many discouraging moments. For example, I realized that I couldn't stay in New York on my aunt's couch forever. Point of the story is: Eloquence was birthed from my experiences of interning for others. From the process, I gained so much knowledge and understanding that has helped me in my own business! Never underestimate the power of giving your time and energy through internships. When you give to others, you will be rewarded and it's not always with the physical dollar bill!

Ask yourself this question. If you could do anything in life that you didn't get paid to do, what would it be? If you can answer this, then you have just revealed a part of your purpose. Once you start walking in it, everything else will fall into place. Every business and project you start will line up to what it is that you love doing. It's like putting the pieces of a puzzle together. I am often amazed at how in tune every thing that I've done in the past 3 years lines up with my purpose. Once yours does, you will know it too!

Three years later, my purpose is still evolving. It's a continuous thing and it just doesn't happen overnight.

Things to Do:

- Sit back and think of all of the things that you love doing. Then ask yourself, "Could I make money doing these things?"

- If you could do anything in this world without pay, what would it be?

- Take out a sheet of paper and begin making a list of these things. Circle the things that are similar. Nine times out of ten, these are the things that you have a passion for!

Chapter Two

Don't Quit Your Day Job...YET!

I know! I know! I'm asking a lot right? However, out of all the great things that you will learn in this book, this is probably the most important one, so pay attention! As my good friend DJ Demp says, "*It's cheaper to pay attention!*" Now I know I speak for most of you when I say this. When you get your first entrepreneurial thought, your confidence goes through the roof! You immediately want to walk away from your day job. "See ya later, alligator!" While this may seem like the time is right, it is not the route to take at the moment and it's definitely not the smartest move to make!

For years, calling it quits with my dreadful 9-5 was one of my heart's biggest desires. I wanted to stay at home and chase all of my dreams and goals. I couldn't wait until I no longer had to punch someone else's clock. Listen carefully...this is not what you want to do! Believe it or not, for many reasons you need your job. Contrary to what some may feel, think or say, holding on to your day job is necessary for financial, personal and professional reasons. I often hear people use the excuse of having a day job as the reason why they can't start their own business. That is exactly what I just said it was, an excuse.

The first thing that you must do while working your full-time job is to be faithful and committed to your employer. You must realize your purpose for being there are both monetarily and professionally. Though you know you are there temporarily, having the best attitude and giving your employer the best service possible is crucial to your future success. You may not love the job you do, but no one should ever know! You must perform your tasks and duties with excellence, no questions asked! Even if you have to pretend! One of the things that I've learned is that how you do one thing is how you will do everything, and this reflects in your attitude. This means, if you go to work with a horrible attitude, how do you think you will approach your own business when you are able to do it full-time? While at your job, it is so important that you keep a positive attitude and try your best to give it your best. We don't know who we will meet or have to serve from day to day. If you go to work with a negative attitude, you could very well meet the person(s) that could have the answers for your own business.

Another reason you need not give up your job at this point is because you will need financial security. There's no worst feeling than to be pursuing your passion and be completely broke, especially if you are physically and mentally able to work. I know this first hand because that was my experience starting out. I sat at home wishing a money tree would miraculously grow in my back yard. Finally, reality hit me. I realized that I needed to get out and find a day job. At least that could help take care of some of my basic needs. Any amount would be a help to finance the start of my business. Yes, living at home freed me from some of the financial responsibilities and pressures that would have made it more difficult for me to build my business. I soon found a job at a local bank and the hours were perfect! Although most of my time during the week would be consumed, I still got off early enough and had evenings and weekends to push my business.

Having a job didn't mean I made tons of money, but I made enough to take care of my personal bills *(cell phone, etc.).* This advantage took some of the burden off of me while transitioning from working a full-time job to becoming my own boss. Finding ways to make extra income also contributed, while taking advantage of opportunities when it presented itself. For instance, if the company offered overtime, I worked as many extra hours as possible. This extra cash came in handy when it was time to purchase my domains, take business trips and even get this book out to the world!

It is equally important while working your

day job, that you work your plan by taking steps each day so that you are closer to leaving. Don't just work your 9-5 job and expect things to come to you. You MUST strategically step towards your freedom. Look at your job as if you are just passing through. It's a temporary position preparing you for your CEO hat at your own company. I once read a quote from Oprah that said, *"Doing the best in this moment puts you in the best place for the next moment."* With that being said, love your day job....if you work it right, you won't be there forever!

• Do a self-evaluation of your attitude towards your day job. If it's poor, clean it up! You won't get far. If it's good, keep smiling, your way of escape is closer than you think!

• Do you have an extra day during the week that you can work overtime or even get a small side job? Go for it! These extra funds can finance those business cards that you need!

• Have some overtime hours this week? Great! Use some of this money to purchase your domain! GoDaddy.com can get you up and running with a free email address for less than 20 bucks!

Chapter Three
Find Ways to Fulfill Your Purpose Monetarily

Now for the good stuff! Money! But don't get too excited just yet. There won't be tons of it flowing in at first. You have to find ways of discovering how to get the money and where the money is. The great news is that while you are working your 9 to 5 job, you can be using your free time to make money doing what you love. For example, once I determined that my purpose was helping other aspiring entrepreneurs discover and start their businesses, I spent my free time setting up websites, getting business cards, creating look books and the list can go on. Although I wasn't making top dollars for my services yet, the money I did bring in was extra cash that allowed me to invest in making my business better. At first, you will have to treat your business like a side hustle. The more you do it and get the experience, you can start charging more and the quality of your business will increase. The key to finding money is a continuous flow of new and better ideas.

In Genesis, it talks about the river that flowed from Eden. That river was divided into four branches for the purpose of watering the garden (Genesis 2:10). I believe the true meaning of this scripture contradicts what many people have been taught in reference to our wealth. In life, we have been taught to solely rely on one source of income *(our 9 to 5 jobs)*. What I believe Genesis 2:10 is saying, is that God created the river to produce more, so that it could create four different streams. He also created and designed us with the same creative power to create several streams of income. We should never have to live in lack and poverty because His plan was for us to always have more than enough. As an entrepreneur, we should have several streams of income because when one vanishes, we will have others to fall back on.

Discovering your purpose is often the greatest challenge. Once that's discovered, think of ways to use your gifts and talents to create revenue in as many ways as possible. Your mind expands and has the creative power to create new and innovative ways and ideas. While working my regular job and running Eloquence Enterprises, I also developed a t-shirt line that cost zero dollars to maintain. That was three sources of income. You get the point?

When I started Eloquence, no one knew who I was or what I had to offer. This made it difficult for potential clients to trust me enough to pay for my services. I had to prove to myself and to others that I was capable of creating a finished product before clients came knocking my door down. I call this the *"show and prove"* method. Before you start pursuing clients and customers, take one of the services that you are offering, and do a dummy project with it. Make sure that you have given this project 150% and showcase it on your own website, Facebook page and blog. This will show potentials what you can do and chances are that you will start to get some business. To this day, whenever I do any of my own graphics, websites, etc., I make sure that I screen shot it and post it for others to see.

There is one simple method that you can use that requires little energy. This method will not only get your name out into the marketplace, but money will begin to flow in your business. Take 20 business cards with you when you leave the house in the mornings. Don't return home until you have passed out all of those cards. When you go to church or the bar for happy hour this weekend, take advantage of the crowd that's usually there. Many of these customers have careers and are frequently open to trying new types of products and services.

It really doesn't matter what your business is. Rather it be hair, makeup or photography, there are always creative and innovative ways that you can make money at any stage of your career. Like I said before, no excuses! Now you may be wondering how you can do this, which brings me to the next topic, thinking outside of the box!

In order to do what's never been done, you have to start thinking how others aren't thinking! Think of one goal that you are trying to accomplish. Nine times out of ten, there are a quarter million others reaching for that same exact goal! To stand apart from the competition, you need to adapt to the "not so obvious" way of thinking. Take the roads that most won't take or even try to avoid, and your business will most likely survive!

A great example that comes to mind is the rapid growth of online stores, or as some may call it "Instagram Boutiques." It seems that each time I log on, there is a new one. However, it doesn't excite me enough to actually click on their profiles and why? Because every store is selling the same products! The possibility of these type businesses lasting is very minimal! At first you may be able to sell to people that you know, but what if they can get it for a better price at another online store? Then you just lost a customer. In these cases, thinking outside of the box is the lifeline to keeping your business open. Since there are so many others like yours out there, finding ways to set your business apart from the competition is important. Making sure that your photos are authentic, not copied, and having an actual website for potential customers to visit are just a couple things you can do to stand out. Reinventing the wheel will always make your business exciting and help produce the money needed to be successful.

Things to Do:

- Be clear on what products and services you have to offer. Once you know this, seek out potential clients and customers and offer it to them.

- Let's practice the "show and prove" method! Think of a service that you offer. Make sure that it is one of your best and do a dummy project. Once you have done this, showcase it by snapping a screen shot and post it on your blog, website and social media sites.

- If you are selling a product, practice thinking outside of the box by finding new and creative ways to showcase what you are selling. Think of something that you haven't done or used already.

Chapter Four
Social Media is the Key
to Creating Your Brand's Identity

Okay, so now you have a business idea or a product, but no one knows about it except your friends and family back in the neighborhood. Trust me when I tell you, that business or product won't get off the ground! In order for people to know who you are and what you have to offer, you have to go out there and interact where they are; and everyone is on social media!

We live in an age where social media has become a very important factor in all aspects of any business. With the huge variety of social media outlets available to us, it has become so much easier to gain contacts, find potential customers, create and maintain our image(s). When you are starting up your business and trying to build a brand, one of the easiest ways *(and did I mention free)* to get your name out there is to hop on Facebook or Twitter and start sharing your goodies *(not literally...lol)*!

I can recall signing up for a Twitter account in 2009. Like many of you, I was so confused and didn't quite get the point of "tweeting." Since then, it's become a part of my daily routine and I've figured out a way to make it work for me.

When I first started tweeting, Facebook was still the most popular social media platform, so there weren't too many people using Twitter. I had no idea what I was doing and had no goals in mind except to send out pointless 140 character messages about my life. At the time, it didn't make much sense, but I'm glad I stuck with it and learned how to use it. Fast forward to today, I'm now probably one of the biggest social media advocates, and it's not just because everyone is doing it. Social media is the factor that lies behind many of my connections and successes.

I could go on and on about the many doors that have opened for me through social media, but I'll save that for another book! However, I would like to share a couple of stories on how Twitter changed the dynamics of my career. Let me begin with the story of when I was in search of finding fashion styling opportunities. I had searched and searched Google time and time again for internships because I knew I needed hands on experience. Unfortunately, I wasn't able to find any that didn't require previous experience. It wasn't until I hopped on Twitter one day and started following all of the top celebrity stylists that I admired. I will never forget one in particular who sent out a tweet that she was looking for an intern in the New York area. I immediately jotted down her email address and submitted my resume. I didn't live in New York and I had no experience at all. A couple of months later, she emailed me and asked me to give her a call. My heart jumped out of my chest! I called her that night and she explained the details of the internship and asked me if I lived in New York. I told her I did not, but I could get there if she gave me the position! Talk about ambition! Long story short, she told me that she would call me back in a few weeks when she got back in the country. By that time, I had already packed my bags and got a one way ticket to New York City. Sadly, when I arrived I never heard from her again. I know you are probably saying, "Aww," but don't, this was a valuable lesson that showed me the power of Twitter and that I could use it to my advantage, only if I learned how to work it.

Another story that comes to mind when thinking of social media opportunities was the time that I was into public relations. Like styling, I needed experience so I hopped on my most trusted sidekick, Twitter and got to searching. I had followed Monique Jackson and Kita Williams who were publicists from the VH1 reality show, "The T.O. Show." They sent out a tweet that they were looking for interns to join their Define Your Pretty group. As you probably already guessed, I jumped on the opportunity and submitted my resume and letter of interest. Months later, I received an email from Monique that said they were going to do a conference call with of the applicants. Although I hadn't landed the internship yet, I was super excited! After several "initiation" calls, I made the final cut in the end. I was now an intern for two of the most powerful women publicist in the industry. Fast forward to today, I am still connected to these two ladies. As a matter of fact, as I'm typing this sentence, I'm on the phone with Monique! I'll later get into the importance of maintaining relationships.

Like I said before, those are just a couple examples of how powerful social media can be. Don't run from it, learn how to use it. Now I'm not saying that social media is the only way to go, but it can be one of the easiest ways to start branding yourself and your business. Here are a few tips that can help you to get the most out of social media:

- *Be sure that your profile photo is the same on all of your social media platforms. Consistency is key in branding!*
- *Interact with others! The most non-productive thing you can do as an entrepreneur is to be mute. Tweet your followers, join in on Facebook conversations, repost Instagram messages and share interesting posts with your LinkedIn connects!*
- *Use search tools and hashtags to find out what your target audience is talking about! Once you do this, you can use this as an opportunity to discuss your business and possibly gain a new customer, client or business partner.*
- *Unprotect your tweets! No need for a long*

explanation: If the world can't see or read your tweets, how will they know if they want to interact with you? If you insist on protecting your tweets, I would suggest creating a personal profile.

- Start with the basics. Create a Facebook and Twitter profile so that you can connect with potential clients and customers. These platforms will also allow you to showcase your products and services professionally.

- Make frequent updates on your profiles. This shows consistency.

- Make sure your updates are professional if your goal is to attract customers and business partners.

Chapter Five

Network with Strategy

If you want to start your own business, you are going to need contacts. In the world of business, connecting with others will become apart of your everyday life. There is absolutely no way around it. Now that that's been established, it's also important to realize that people are different and they lead different lives. Some are much easier to connect with than others. I learned that those that may seem impossible to connect with *(i.e.: a celebrity)*, go to the next best thing! By this I mean, contact that person's assistant, publicist, manager, or even take a look at that person's timeline and see who they interact with the most! This confirms why tweeting is a must. By connecting with the people closest to the person that you are ultimately trying to connect with, will make your chances much greater.

Networking ties in with thinking outside of the box. I remember when I was a public relations intern for Celebrity Fashion Stylist, Tiffany Dean and her mom's popular fashion design company, Deanzign. We had just introduced a new line of jersey dresses and as their intern my job was to seek out top celebrities to wear the dresses. During that time, the Wendy

Williams Show was becoming one of the most popular shows on air. I knew if I could just get her to wear one of the dresses for publicity, I would be in the game! What I thought would be the hard part was actually getting in touch with her. Although I knew if I sent out enough emails and tweets someone would respond, I decided to take another route. I went to Google and found out who her wardrobe stylist was at the time. To confirm this information, I watched the Wendy Williams Show all that week and zoomed in on the end credits! Once I gathered this information, I was able to get her stylist's contact. It wasn't long after that show aired I got a response! Not only was I able to get her stylist to agree to dress Wendy in the new jersey dresses, but Wendy fell in love with them and they became her "go to "dress for the rest of the season! You see, it's totally possible to connect with anyone that you dream of. You just have to be strategic in your networking.

Now to the big question, what are some ways to network and get the most out of it? First of all, networking and how often you do it shouldn't depend on your location. You can network both on and offline. A lot of times it is easy to assume that you can't interact with others in your field of interest because you don't live in a big city. Starting off by finding out what's happening in your local area is always a smart idea. You'd be surprised at how many other individuals that have similar interests right in your own town! Seek out any upcoming events where others with like minds will attend and make sure that you are in attendance as well. Several cities have occasional events such as mixers, group meetings, showcases and the list can go on. Now while it may seem smart to attend every event possible, try working smarter and not harder. Only attend events that will be beneficial to you building your business. As an entrepreneur, time is valuable so you don't want to spend your time at an event that has nothing to do with your vision.

When attending events, make sure that you step in the door with confidence. Lack thereof will stick out like a sore thumb! Know your business and what you have to offer because someone will ask. It is also important to know the art of "small talk." Knowing your elevator speech is important. When asked who you are you should be able to introduce yourself and your business in 30 seconds or less. When you meet someone, rather it is face to face or on social media, chatting about something other than the business can help spark up the conversation that you are looking for.

Now another important aspect of networking that I've learned over the years. It's what I call keeping a *"contact bank."* This means that if you meet someone through networking, it may not result in an immediate connection. Don't just toss their business card and conversation into the trash can. I guarantee that you will be able to come back to that person some where in the future. Never throw away a contact, just stick it in your contact bank for later use. This brings me to the next topic, building and maintaining relationships.

Things to Do:

- Here's a quick exercise! Think of one person that you would love to connect with but think it will be difficult to reach them. Take out your notepad and jot down a list of people that you think are closest to them on their team and start doing your research! I can almost guarantee you that you can reach one of them, especially via social media.

- Save and organize your contacts. You can do this by creating a spreadsheet or list in Microsoft Excel, Access or Word. Categorizing them by profession, city/state and even note how you connected will make it a lot more useful!

- Open your local newspaper or hop on Facebook to find an industry event to attend.

Chapter Six

Build & Maintain Relationships

Building and maintaining relationships with others is very important in both our personal and professional lives. Think about the relationships that you have with your parents, siblings or significant other. Nine times out of ten, you cherish those relationships enough by making sure that you nurture and care for them. Attending family dinners, making date nights priority and so on are all ways to do this. What you are actually doing is making yourself available by spending time with the people that are important in your life. The same principles apply when building and maintaining business relationships. The true reality is, we all need people and relationships.

It is impossible to start and build any business all on your own. While the ideas and majority of the hard work may come from you, you still need help from others. It is through your connection with others that opens the doors to get your business started. As you journey through life, you will find out that there are several types of relationships in business and you must cherish and maintain each one. Every one of them has some value and type of influence in your life. A relationship can either lift you up or weigh you down. As you build your business, you will have relationships with other entrepreneurs, potential business partners, clients and customers. Sometimes you will interact with these individuals on a daily, monthly or even yearly basis. This all depends on each person's schedule, projects, location, etc. No matter the situation, it is important that you keep the connection open in all of your relationships.

Over the years, I've come into contact with people from many different walks of life. I've had the privilege of interacting with people in the fashion, media, beauty and entertainment industries. Some I correspond with daily, monthly, over a year's time, and some only once or twice! No matter what the frequency of the encounters, it is okay because flexibility and variety allows me to discern if someone can add to the building of my business. As I stated in the previous chapter, every individual that you come into contact with, may not seem beneficial at that time. The bottom line is, in order to keep the line of communication open, you must build a relationship. Now I'm not saying to call them up on a daily basis, but it does help if you stay in the loop of what's going on within both their personal and professional lives. You can easily do this by simply following them on social media and remembering their birthday.

The key to building and maintaining

relationships is communication. The only way to build a relationship with someone is to interact with them. This can be achieved in many ways such as through telephone, email, text messages, video chats, and the list can go on and on. Whichever method of communication you choose will depend on the type of relationship that you are building with someone. The stronger and more mature you are as an individual, the more likely you will seek and attract friends and associates who have similar traits and qualities. However, it is so important to not get caught up in the fad of being a copy cat. The authenticity of your brand or business depends on you being comfortable in your own skin.

Lastly, communication in a healthy relationship also comes through transparency. Your business can benefit significantly if you are in relationships that are "win-win". This means that you should always evaluate who will serve and support you, as well as who you will serve and support. You can only win if those in relationships are transparent and honest with you and you with them. These are the healthy relationships that will make both parties happy, fulfilled and safe. Watch out for "wannabes!" We should always strive for the best, but beware of those who talk the talk but are not walking the walk. It is extremely important to always let your word have weight and let it mean what it says. Don't make promises you can't keep. After all, saying "no" is better than a "yes" that can't be kept!

Remember building and maintaining relationships is key in building your brand, business or career. The type of relationships that you develop begins with you. As you build them, you will discover what each one means to you. Being honest about who you are is the key ingredient to an authentic brand or business that sticks out like none other. Remember, healthy relationships can help build a strong and healthy business.

Things to Do:

- Pull out the contact list that you created in the last chapter. Be sure to add birthdays to these contacts if you have that information. You can even set an alert on your phone next to each of your contacts name so that when their birthday comes, you can send them a quick tweet, text or email!

Chapter Seven
Adopt a "Do-It-Yourself" Attitude

This chapter actually covers how I _could_ start my business with no money. I had to do what I had to do myself, which included the things I didn't know how to do. I had to research and learn because I did not have the money to pay anyone. One of the most common reasons why most aspiring entrepreneurs don't start their own business is because they automatically think that they don't have the money needed to invest in what they need. Well, that may be true, but that does not have to be the reason you stop. Let me reiterate! Once again, this is nothing more than an invalid excuse that we most often make without actually realizing it. We are so used to assuming that you need thousands of dollars to get the basic things to start a _business (i.e.: website, business cards, logo, etc.)_ until we are ultimately missing out...BIG TIME! How on earth can you start a business with that mindset? You must adapt a "do-it-yourself" attitude and figure out exactly how you can get what you need without kicking out any money upfront. Even if you are an established business owner and entrepreneur, having this attitude can be very beneficial. It can save you tons of money, enhance your portfolio and save you the time and energy of hiring any employees early on. It is totally possible!

When I started my business, I learned how to do EVERYTHING! It wasn't because I wanted to create a career or hobby out of it. It was because I didn't have the money to pay anyone to do what I could possibly do myself. Since I spent most of my free time interning for other companies and entrepreneurs, I took what I learned and applied it to building my own business and brand. I gained experience in just about every area such as public relations, administrative work and graphics. I applied those experiences, did some additional research, and made it happen all on my own!

As a beginner, I believe that every entrepreneur should learn the basics in each of the following categories: public relations, graphic and website design, basic management and social media management skills. You should know how to correspond to your own emails, maintain your own blog, and pitch yourself or company to your favorite magazine. Who do you think pitched me to be featured in "Today's Black Woman" Magazine? Well, I don't have a publicist, so I used the skills that I gained from working in public relations previously to pitch my own self! You can do it too!

This same "do-it-yourself" attitude allowed me to create and design all of my websites, logos, and stationary that I use for Eloquence

Enterprises and The Tottie Brand. The only money that I spent was for the domains. Talk about money saved! There are several resources online that can help you to get the necessary materials needed to get your business started. You can do all of this during the weekend or your free time when you are not clocked in at your 9-5. Here are a few that I've used in the past that are great money savers!

Websites: Wix, Google Sites, On Sugar

Business Cards: Vistaprint, Zazzle

Logo & other Graphics: Pic Monkey, Logo Maker, Logo Creator

Social Media Management: Hootsuite, Social Oomph, Tweet Deck, Sprout Social

Well, I know that there are still some doubting the possibility of starting a business with 0 dollars. You may be saying, *"I don't have internet connection. You have to pay for that!"* If you are in a situation where internet isn't available, there are many places that have free internet access. The library, restaurants, coffee shops and other public places that we visit on a daily basis all has free Wi-Fi. It all depends on how anxious and passionate you are about starting your brand, business or career. To be honest, I have even sat in my car to get free internet on several occasions. It really boils down to how bad you want it! You can do whatever you need to do with no money. It's possible, if you don't give up. Learning to improvise is the key in making the impossible happen.

Barter Your Own Skills & Services

Now if you just absolutely have to hire a professional or someone that knows what they are doing to create your website, design your logo, etc., don't be so quick to shuck out the Benjamins! There are ways that you can barter your own skills and services with another professional or aspiring entrepreneur. Barter means "to exchange goods or services for other goods or services without using money." In other words, if you are good at designing websites, but are horrible at writing a press release, reach out to an aspiring public relations entrepreneur who is just starting out and negotiate! Then you could barter by offering the other individual your website design services in exchange for him/her writing your press release. By doing this you are saving money but also getting what you need for your business! Utilize social media and Craigslist to find out who's willing to barter their skills and services. It is a very effective method of networking without doing it physically.

Things to Do:

- Need business cards? Hop on your laptop or smart phone and go to www.Vistaprint.com. Click on Business Cards and make your own cards! This website usually runs specials on business cards so take advantage. Sometimes it could cost as little as 0 dollars. You only pay for the shipping!

- Think of something that you need to start your business (i.e.: website or logo). Hop on Facebook and update your status asking for recommendations for anyone that can do what you need. Network and find someone who is starting out just like you and negotiate your services!

Chapter Eight

READ, READ, READ...
What? EVERYTHING!

Okay, now I know you think that this step is one that you can *(and probably will)* skip over, but please don't. Reading is the key to so many doors when starting and building the business and brand of your dreams. While most may feel that reading stops at high school finals, it is even more important now than it's ever been. Most of the time, the answer to that question you've been asking about your industry and business all lies in the pages of a book. However, the only way to find that answer is to open a book and read.

In today's world, reading has never been easier, and might I add more convenient! You don't have to visit your local bookstore or library anymore; just simply hop on your laptop, iPad or smart phone and you have millions of reading materials right at your fingertips. It's important to get into the habit of reading books as well as other reading materials such as magazines and blogs. You would be surprised that these resources hold just as much information as a 100 page book.

Reading books and other resources that focus on your specific industry and business is important. However, opening books on other topics like, how to write a press release or how to market a product are all also very helpful. You can never learn or know too much! Soak in as much information as you can because it will all contribute to the success of your business. It is vital that you know as much as you can about the business you are starting. Obviously you won't know every little detail, but making it a priority to stay in the know of what's going on can put you ahead of the competition. Knowledge is power and you hold the key to making sure that your business has meaning and impact in the world.

Thinking back, if I hadn't picked up Kim Maxwell's book on fashion styling, I wouldn't have known that I needed to find internships to gain experience. I know that I would have learned this eventually, but you know what they say, there's no time like the present! What I found in the pages of this book, not only provided me with insight into my career interest, but it also gave me hope. Hope to know that I could find out just what I needed to know about starting my business, all within the confinements of something so simple, a book.

- Make a short list of all of the questions that you have about starting up your business. Go to Amazon.com and type in the topic of your question and find a book that covers this information.

- Download iBook or Kindle and have a book on hand to read during your free time.

- On your lunch breaks, skim through the latest magazines and log on to your favorite blogs as it pertains to your business/industry.

Chapter Nine
Use Google, It's Your Best Friend

I am often blasted with emails, messages and tweets asking me about what resources or contacts I use. Now don't get me wrong, I love helping others in any way that I can. However, over the last three or four years, I've had many sleepless and might I add broke nights. When I needed to research, I used the only resource that I had available, the world's most popular search engine, Google. Coming into the business, I didn't know anything and had no one to call up and ask. I had to use the only free resource that I had at the time. As I've stated many times in the previous chapters, it is so important that you learn how to use what's available right at your finger tips. Google is the most obvious resource if you learn how to use it properly.

Now I know you may be thinking, "Natasha, *ANYONE* can use Google." Yes, this is true. However, there's a huge difference between using Google and using it effectively. Time is important, so once again, don't waste your time scrolling through pages and pages of search results before you find what you are looking for. To make your Google search easier, there are a few different search tools and categories that you can put to use.

Google allows you to search by web, images, videos, etc. You can also sort the results by date, which is one of my favorite tools! Searching by the date will determine how relevant what you are searching is to the current date. Let me give you an example. Let's say you were looking for step-by-step instructions on how to set up your WordPress blog for your business. Go to Google and type in "how to set up a WordPress blog." You will then get a list of results that include articles, video clips, images and more. Since you are looking for step-by-step instructions, the easiest way would be to actually watch how to set your blog up. You would then click on the "Videos" option so that your results are filtered to just video clips. It's that simple, especially if you are a visual learner. This is just one way to use Google effectively.

Another common way to do an effective Google search is to think about exactly what you are looking for. If you need a picture, simply select "Images" and instead of getting results in text, you will get all images instead. Easy huh? The same rules apply if you are looking for a video clip or a news report. I could go on and on about the many ways to use the search tools. However, the best way to learn is to play around with them and find the ones that work best for you.

When doing your Google search, using keywords is also important. Truth is, all search engines are powered by keywords. Keywords are those "stand out" words or "key" words that search engines use to give you results. I won't take up your time explaining search engines and SEOs because that's a subject that can take days! As a matter of fact, Google it! Any word can be a keyword but if it has nothing to do with what you are searching for, it's pointless to use it in your search. For example, if I wanted to look up "how to organize a fashion show," the key words in this search would be "organize" and "fashion show." You see, they are the main words in the search.

As with anything else, practice makes perfect! Take some time to practice doing an effective Google search and compare it to how you have been doing it before. I can almost guarantee that you will get more accomplished and find more information in less time!

Things to Do:

- Make a list of three things that you need to know in order to start your business. Start with the first one and Google it.

- Be sure to identify keywords in your previous searches.

- Play around with the different search tools in your previous searches.

Chapter Ten
Stay True to Your Vision
& Don't Compromise It

Often times this is much easier said than done. In a world where it seems like all the great ideas have been taken, it is so easy to lose focus of what your vision is for your own business. I would say it's more of a subconscious thing. Most industries are so overly saturated, until everyone is doing the same things, selling the same products and slapping a different name on it. Well, to each it's own, but I can guarantee you that those businesses don't last.

This is where staying true to your vision is vital. Yes, it's true that there are seven billion people in this world. However, each and every one of us has a vision that is hand crafted and specifically designed for us. No matter how hard it may seem or how familiar your vision is to someone else's, it's yours! Don't let fear of failure and unacceptance sneak in and allow you to get off track. Carry out your vision just the way it was given to you, because this is the only way that your business will thrive. This goes back to the chapter on relationships. The authenticity of your vision depends on your uniqueness. Being proud and loving who you are will produce a business, brand or career you can be proud of also.

There is a famous saying, "no pain, no gain." Some times you will feel like throwing in the towel and giving up. There will be occasions when things will not go as planned. My advice to you is never give up. In some cases, you may have to step back, rethink and plan over from a different perspective. I found out that it was when I was put in difficult situations, I was forced to hustle and figure out exactly what I needed to do next. As I continued to persevere, it became easier to accept lessons that were building blocks. It is important to recognize how much energy and attention to give the good, bad and the ugly! Realizing when it is time to move on to the next lesson is a very important factor.

Whenever you feel yourself compromising your vision, take a moment and revaluate what you are doing wrong. Usually it's only a small adjustment that can get you back on track. Remember all of the reasons why you wanted to start your own business in the first place.

Let me take you back and tell you one last story on how my vision was tested and almost compromised. In 2012, after being in New York for about a year, I decided to return home to South Carolina. Although my experiences in the Big Apple were ones that were the foundation of my career, I had run out of money, options and was homesick.

Instead of coming home and getting back in the comforts of "normal," I still aimed to pursue my passions. One of the things I loved and enjoyed about my time in New York were the quality of events and the role that a great event plays in an entrepreneur's life. I can remember getting invited to and attending what would be called "parties" in my home state. However, these weren't just parties. They were more like elaborate, networking events that allowed myself, other industry professionals and wannabes, to congregate under the same roof hoping to make connections.

These types of events were the complete opposite of what I was familiar with. I was used to putting on my tightest and shortest dress, and stepping in some of the most backdoor establishments, mingling with individuals who were just looking for a good time. Now don't get me wrong, this was all good because I enjoyed every one of those nights! However, when you are trying to become a professional and start a business, there must be a method to your madness. In this case, the madness being partying. While in New York, I learned that it is okay to party, but do it in a way that you will benefit.

With that being said, when I came back to

South Carolina I had already become accustomed to this type of entertainment. I figured that just maybe I could bring these experiences back to my home town and so I did just that. I created what was called, "Unmask the Swag," a black tie affair that would allow the urban, trendsetting individual to put on their best attire and join together to mingle in a comfortable environment. The problem was, after working hard to promote the event months prior, not many purchased tickets. When the night of the event came, no one but the deejay and bartender showed up. So many things went wrong. There I was feeling so discouraged because none of my friends or family even came to support what I thought was a good thing. My parents had exhausted all of their money to help me put on this event and there was no return in the investment. Well at least that's what I thought at that time. After the event, I was so hurt and disappointed until we made the 3 ½ hour drive back to where we lived. It took me some time to get over it, but when I wiped away the tears and was able to put this experience behind me, I realized that my intentions behind this event were good. The truth is, the people that I tried to incorporate in my vision just weren't who it was for. They weren't ready for change and I had to accept that and move on.

I later found out that even though my event wasn't the success I wanted it to be, I did make some type of impact after all. Some of the more well- known party-goers in the city came together and "reenacted" the exact same type of event that I attempted to put together! You see, I could have given up and thought that the vision that was given to me was in vain. The end result was that I did bring something new, even if no one ever acknowledged it. I'm so happy that I kept moving forward because my vision, business and brand has expanded and gone to heights that I only imagined. The skies the limit and I have vowed to continue staying true to myself, my business and the brand that God gave to me.

Things to Do:

- Go back to the basics. Think back to the reasons why you wanted to start your own business in the first place.

Conclusion

My hope is that by the time you have reached this page, the habits, methods and principals shared in the preceding pages will help you to start your business. They say experience is the best teacher. I believe that with each story that I've told, each failure that I've endured and every victory that I've won, you will be able to take the basics of how I started my business and apply it to yours.

The sole purpose of this book was to show you how you can kick start your business using no money and very little resources. If you don't continue to find methods and ways to keep your business growing, taking the time to read this book will have served you no justice at all. In order to grow, you must continue to expand your knowledge of business and the industry that you are pursuing. You can't stop at this page.

Entrepreneurship is the new American dream. It's not only empowering this generation to bring dreams to life, but its reward is financial freedom. This is something that I definitely aim for and I'm sure you do to!

Since writing this book, I was laid off from my 9-5! My financial cushion was pulled right up from under me and now I am forced to pursue my passions and dreams full-time! It's been a long road until now. Although I left my day job involuntarily, I am so thankful that I have prepared and took the steps necessary to kick start my business and brand years ago.

Tips to Take from This Book:

- Know your purpose? Great! This is the first step in starting your dream business.

- While you are working your 9-5 day or night job, use your free time (i.e.: weekends, evenings) to work on the essentials needed to present your business to the world.

- Find potential clients/customers in your local city. Start with them. Be sure to keep records by taking photos and sharing your craft/talents.

- Utilize the best free online tool, social media to introduce and build your business platform. Interact with others by creating and utilizing a Facebook, Twitter and Instagram account.

- Make networking a daily habit. Don't miss out on any opportunities because you don't have a business card.

- Work a few hours overtime and use these funds to purchase your website domain, business cards, and more.

- Continue to feed your mind with books and reading resources that will enhance your knowledge of business and the industry in which you are pursuing.

- Don't be afraid to use Google. It's free and can lead you to any information that you would like to know about your business.

- Consistency is the key to a successful business and brand. By staying true to the vision that you have for your business, is what will drive it to greatness.

Acknowledgments

I MADE IT! To the last page of this book that is. I have finally achieved a life-long goal. While I could easily sit here and say I made this happen on my own, I would be telling a lie.

To the number one person in my life, God. You heard my prayers, knew the intensity of the passion in my heartbeat and gave favor to allow me to complete such a major task. I owe you the upmost gratitude.

To my mom, my #1 fan...whew, where do I begin? There just aren't enough pages to express how thankful I am to you for helping me during this season. From caring for my newborn so I could write an extra paragraph to spending hours proofing and editing this book...you have shown me the true definition of love and I could never repay you for it.

To my dad, thank you for always encouraging me to stay busy and to never give up...I love you.

To my siblings, ***El & Trish***...thank you for loving me!

And to my Prince, Tyler...I do this for you!

Special Thanks to: All of my supporters both on and offline – Angel, Regina, Chavis, Loren Ridinger & Market America, Monique Jackson, Kita Williams, Tiffany Dean, Erica Rae, Kendrell Bowman, Aleesha Carter, Khaliah Clark, Sam DeSalu, DJ Demp, Essence Gant, Chris 'DJ Beanz' Lewis, Kim Maxwell, LaToya McLean, Elisha & Gemini Virgin Hair Co., Jake Simpson, Michelle Black & Social Butterfly Boutique, Tanise and Team Tottie.
Thank you for being a part of my journey.

Credits

Google.com
Kim Maxwell, *Career Diary of a Fashion Stylist, 2007*
Bible, *KJV*
DJ Demp, quotation
Oprah Winfrey, quotation
Facebook.com
Twitter.com
Instagram.com
LinkedIn.com
Deanzign
The Wendy Williams Show
Today's Black Woman Magazine
Wix.com
OnSugar.com
Vistaprint.com
Zazzle.com
PicMonkey.com
LogoMaker.com
LogoCreator.com
Hootsuite
Social Oomph
TweetDeck
Sprout Social
Craigslist.com
Amazon.com
Wordpress.com

About the Author

Natasha 'Tottie' Weston is a native of Mount Pleasant, SC and currently resides in Greenville, SC. She is an entrepreneur and founder of Eloquence Enterprises. She is the motivational blogger behind TableTalkwithTottie.com. Most known for her hustler spirit and multi-talents, Natasha is on her way to becoming the next leader in business, social media, entrepreneurship and fashion. As of today, she's been featured in an array of blogs and magazines, contributing her thoughts and ideas on the fashion, business, media and entertainment industries.

Although she is still an intermediate in this game of business, her main priority is to be effective in all that she does. This mogul-in-the-making is building an empire from the ground up by simply creating her own opportunities.

Learn more about Natasha by visiting www.TheTottieBrand.com.

www.ingramcontent.com/pod-product-compliance
Lightning Source LLC
Chambersburg PA
CBHW070826210326
41520CB00011B/2136